YOU WERE ONCE A DREAM

A Reminder That You Are Special

WRITTEN BY
KASSANDRA HAUGHTON

ACKNOWLEGEMENTS

Thank you to my friends and family who listened
continually as I read to you until I knew this story was
ready—particularly my mom, who would have likely
listened another hundred times over. I appreciate
her constant encouragement to keep going.

Thank you to my fellow critique member Robin
and colleague Nickie, who without hesitation offered
their time to read through this book and provide
their words of wisdom, love, and support.

I am grateful to Hameo Pham and her remarkable gift of art.

Mostly, I am thankful to God for sharing His words of love
for a generation of children who need to know
He has been thinking about them for a long time.

I dedicate this book to Jayda.
You are my dream come true.

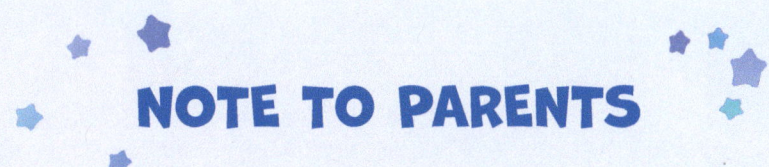

NOTE TO PARENTS

Dear parents, guardians, caregivers, family, and friends,

I believe now more than ever it is essential for our children to know they are not part of this world by chance. There is a Creator who took time and gave incredible thought to their existence. There is a reason and purpose behind each child's birth—even if they cannot see it yet.

As many of us know, children will face challenges throughout their lives that will make them question whether they are really meant to be part of this world. I have written this book as a simple yet powerful reminder that there is no uncertainty about whether we are meant to be here.

I have used Jeremiah 1:5 as the foundation for the words in this book. While I recognize this scripture does not specifically state that God dreamed about us, my aim is to use these words as evidence for young children, that just like Jeremiah, God has given special care and attention to their design. As well, I do not use "dream" to mean God closed His eyes, went to sleep, and dreamed about each and every one of us when we were children, but rather that He had a vision for who each of us would be even before we were born.

I encourage you to build strong and healthy foundations for your child(ren) about how important they are, so that when they are faced with life's questionable moments, they are motivated to persevere because they understand that they are meant to be here.

Lastly, and most importantly, frequently remind your child(ren) that they are loved and carry within them immeasurable value.

I pray for you as you travel on this beautiful parenting journey, caring for a child or simply being present for the children who cross your path. There are so many great things to learn along the way.

Kassandra

JEREMIAH 1:5

"Before I formed you in the womb I knew you . . ."
(Holy Bible, English Standard Version)

You have a purpose.

Before we get started,
I have an important message for you:
God made you special, you are unique, and you are loved
by Him in every single way. You are perfectly you,
and no one can take your place in this world.

Now, I have a few questions for you.

Did you play in the bubbles,
and wash between your toes?

Have you had a bedtime snack,
like some veggies or some fruit?

Have you brushed your teeth, to keep your pearlies looking white?

Did you wash your face?

Are you
snuggled in bed?

Or perhaps
you just
finished playing?

Don't close your eyes just yet.
I have just a few more questions for you,
if you don't mind.

Have you ever wondered
about the color of your eyes?
Your cute little nose?
The brightness of your smile?

Well, you were once a dream:
a beautiful picture in the mind of God.

Before you were born, God pictured in His mind
exactly who you would be and what you would do.

He thought about your eyes, your ears, your nose, and your smile. He knew how tall you would be, what your voice would sound like, and what special gifts He would place on the inside of you.

He thought about the people who would become your family and how much He would want for them to shower you with love.

He didn't just think about you once.
He thought about you over and over and over again.
You were a dream He kept safe in His heart
until just the right time.

And one day, when everything was complete,
and He had perfected every detail,
He decided it was time for you
to become a reality.

God wants you to know
you are one of His most favourite creations.
You are His dream come true.

There may be moments where you
feel imperfect and unsure of what to do.
When this happens, remember that
God has made you perfect
for everything you need to do.

If ever you're feeling sad or alone, send God a prayer.
Whether you whisper or shout, He'll hear every word,
because He is always listening.

Should we take a moment
to say thank you to God
for thinking about you?

Dear God, thank you for creating me exactly how you pictured me to be. Please help me to always remember that I am loved and special, because You love me and created me special and unique. On days when perhaps I do not feel as special as I should, I pray I will remember the things you have created, like the flowers, the birds, and the beautiful skies, and know I am special just the way I am. Thank you for my family and friends. You have made every single one of us perfectly unique. Thank you for dreaming a purpose and a plan for each of us. **Amen.**

Now, sleep tight,
and may you rest in God,
because with Him,
dreams come true.

Sweet Dreams.

Good night.

Psalms 139:13 - 17

New King James Version

For you formed my inward parts;
You covered me in my mother's womb.

I will praise You, for I am fearfully and wonderfully made;
Marvelous are Your works, And that my soul knows very well.

My frame was not hidden from You, When I was made in
secret, And skillfully wrought in the lowest parts of the earth.

Your eyes saw my substance, being yet unformed.
And in Your book they all were written, The days fashioned
for me, When as yet there were none of them.

How precious also are Your thoughts to me, O God!
How great is the sum of them!

FriesenPress

One Printers Way
Altona, MB R0G 0B0
Canada

www.friesenpress.com

ISBN
978-1-03-916335-5 (Hardcover)
978-1-03-916334-8 (Paperback)
978-1-03-916336-2 (eBook)

1. JUVENILE NONFICTION, BEDTIME & DREAMS

Distributed to the trade by The Ingram Book Company

ABOUT THE AUTHOR

Kassandra Haughton is a writer, teacher, dreamer, and parent. She holds a Bachelor of Arts in Psychology and a master's degree in Adult Education. She is passionate about helping people by reminding them that they are important, they have a reason for existing. Her memories of reading bedtime stories with her own mother inspired her to write a bedtime story for the hearts and imaginations of children everywhere. *You Were Once a Dream* is her first book.

Kassandra lives in Regina, Saskatchewan with her family. Learn more at www.kassandrahaughton.com.

Milton Keynes UK
Ingram Content Group UK Ltd.
UKHW050426171123
432730UK00002B/18